30 DAYS TO HAPPINESS

Daily Meditations and Actions for Finding True Joy Within Yourself

RHONDA SCIORTINO

Hatherleigh Press is committed to preserving and protecting the natural resources of the earth. Environmentally responsible and sustainable practices are embraced within the company's mission statement.

Visit us at www.hatherleighpress.com and register online for free offers, discounts, special events, and more.

30 Days to Happiness

Library of Congress Cataloging-in-Publication Data is available.
ISBN: 978-1-57826-782-8

Printed in the United States
10 9 8 7 6 5 4 3 2

COVER AND INTERIOR DESIGN BY CAROLYN KASPER

CONTENTS

This book is dedicated to all the people who struggle with depression and to all those who suffer from the depression of the people they love. The good news is that we can actively fight depression by creating and enjoying our genuine happiness.

INTRODUCTION

E verybody wants to be happy, yet few people know *how* to achieve this elusive goal. We think we will be happy if we get the right job, have the right people in our lives, get a new car, and so on. But the problem with this mindset is that, if we only feel happiness when we have what we want, we will *never* be happy—because there will *always* be something else we want. Genuine happiness isn't found in achievements or in the acquisition of material things. All of those things may feel good for a time, but the newness eventually wears off and the happy feelings fade.

Real happiness isn't tied to anything outside ourselves, so when we allow our happiness to be contingent on other people or circumstances, we're giving up our control. When we give up control, our lives become a never-ending emotional roller coaster ride. When things go well, we're happy; when they don't, we're depressed. When people treat us well, we're happy; when people are unfair or rude, we're angry or sad.

What's more, putting the responsibility for our happiness on other people is far too much for them to have to bear. The only person who is truly responsible for your happiness is *you*.

Let's consider what authentic happiness really is. It is not solely a feeling; feelings are superficial and can change from one moment to the next. Genuine happiness is something much deeper—a sense of contentedness, the certain knowledge that despite whatever may be wrong in the world, all is well with our soul.

When we reach that level of peace, our happiness becomes joy. Joy is different and distinct from happiness, as joy is truly internal. It isn't affected by external circumstances. When our happiness becomes joy, we can carry it with us even into the worst turmoil, thereby bringing peace into discord, rather than turmoil and discord disrupting our peace.

Before we can reach that level of joy and inner peace, we must first find our own authentic happiness. And to do that, we must determine what currently stands in the way of our being happy. If you want to get happy and stay happy, rather than just vaguely hoping that it'll eventually happen "someday," you must choose to deliberately pursue, attain, and maintain authentic happiness.

To do that, there are six steps you must follow:

1. Choose positivity
2. Take an honest assessment of your current level of happiness
3. Decide what you want to change
4. Determine what you will need in order to live the consistently happy life you want to live
5. Decide how to best get from where you are now to where you want to be
6. Take a step *every day* to get where you want to go

While birthdays, year's ends, and other times of transition (like job loss, divorce, retirement, etc.) are ideal times to step back, take inventory, and prepare for your future, these steps can be taken at any time. All it takes is a willingness to improve, a commitment to your own well-being, and an actionable plan to get you to where you want to be.

The important thing is that instead of measuring "stuff," we'll be measuring what truly counts—the intangibles, such as relationships, love, and character traits.

The true measure of genuine happiness is in these five points:

- Good relationships
- Good health
- Peace
- Joy
- Financial provision

Achieving one of the facets of success without the others can never lead to the fullness of authentic happiness that accompanies real success. For example, the notion of equating wealth with success is false. There are many financially prosperous people who are miserable. When people destroy their health while trying to earn wealth, they typically don't enjoy the journey, and they aren't able to freely enjoy what they earn. When people fail to invest time in quality relationships while trying to earn wealth, they aren't able to enjoy their wealth through the kind of friendships that typically take years to develop. Once a person becomes wealthy, it is difficult to develop authentic, trusting relationships with people with whom they can enjoy their wealth. Think of the five facets of real success as the foundational pillars of an authentically happy life.

In creating your action plan for a truly successful life, take inventory of the things of true value in your life. If you are courageous enough to do this raw assessment, you will have gathered all the data you need to make deliberate decisions about what you will need to do to improve your happiness and your life.

Throughout this book you will gain rich wisdom and practical tips for acquiring and guarding your happiness. You will learn the secrets about how listening can increase your happiness, and how failure to really listen can steal it away. You will learn how the character traits of courage, honesty, and reliability can help you lead a happier life. And you will gain the wisdom that every truly happy person knows about how your choices to be positive, fair, and creative will lead to real, sustainable happiness.

30 Days to Happiness is an honest assessment of the 30 "life inventory items" that have the biggest influence on your happiness. Let the next 30 days represent a fresh beginning—a "do-over" of sorts, only this time you'll have more experience and greater wisdom than ever before.

You can assess previous plans that didn't work out, mine the lessons out of difficult experiences, make adjustments, and try again without beating yourself up. Thomas Edison tried thousands of times before inventing the incandescent lightbulb. Adjusting your approach and trying again is what eventually leads to success. Giving up never does!

DAY 1
LOVE

*"Love is that condition in which the happiness
of another person is essential to your own."*
—ROBERT A. HEINLEIN

LOVE is the very first, and most important, life inventory item.

The problem with love in our culture is that it is ill-defined. We say that we love ice-cream, we love our pets, and our new outfit; and then we say that we love our family and friends. Throwing around the word 'love' diminishes its depth and significance. Of course, the love we feel for those dearest to our hearts is clearly different than those other things that we enjoy and appreciate; yet we struggle to fully articulate the distinction.

Authentic love is measured in several ways, with the most significant being actions. Actions speak louder than words. For example, if a person says, "*I love you*," but their actions include verbal and/or physical mistreatment, those actions reflect the truth that the person's words are disingenuous, or are evidence that the person doesn't understand the true meaning of love.

Indicators of authentic love include kindness, gentleness, consideration, humility, selflessness, believing the best of people, and defending loved ones. Notice that "feelings" aren't included in this list of indicators of genuine love. While feelings certainly are a part of the true meaning of love, they can also be a false indicator and shouldn't be relied on solely. You can have very strong feelings of love for someone one minute and have very different feelings after that person says or does something that you find unacceptable.

To be truly happy, it's important that we have love in our life. This doesn't mean that we must be *in* love or that we must wait around for someone to show up and love us before we can be happy. We can begin right now—right where we are—to *give* love to those around us. There shouldn't be a qualification process for determining why, when, how and to whom we give love. The beautiful thing about love is that we feel happier when we give it as well as when we receive it. So give it freely through acts of loving kindness while expecting nothing in return. Just give love for the sake of love, and with every genuine act of unconditional kindness your happiness will increase!

Take an honest look at the love you've shared throughout the past year. Ask yourself: have you shown love to yourself and to others? Have you withheld love until others "deserve" it, or have you given it expecting nothing in return?

Meditation

Authentic love changes me, those around me, and our circumstances.

Actions

- I will show at least one unconditional act of love (expecting nothing in return—not even a "thank you") to the people closest to me within the next seven days.

- I will not withhold love, or the kindness that accompanies it, from others—even when I feel that they don't "deserve" it.

- I will overlook the things I don't like about others and love them, flaws and all.

- I will not express my love solely in words. I will make sure that my actions match my words.

The amount of love you feel increases with the amount of love that you give to yourself and to others. *You get "extra credit" for showing love to those who can do nothing to you or for you.*

On a scale of 1–10, 10 being highest, how would you rate yourself for love given to yourself? For love given to others? How will you increase your happiness by showing love for yourself and for others?

DAY 2
RELATIONSHIPS

"Whoever is happy will make others happy."
—Anne Frank

RELATIONSHIPS provide strong indicators for the quality of our lives. The simple truth is that good relationships make us feel good and bad relationships make us feel badly. Review the relationships you have with the people in every area of your life. Do you have at least one relationship with someone who is loyal, trustworthy, and can be called upon in times of trouble? Are you that person for at least one other?

If you get disappointed, upset, frustrated, or angry when things don't go the way you'd hoped (and who doesn't?), rather than automatically plunging into sadness or anger and directing your negative emotions toward whoever let you down (or worse, everyone in your vicinity), ask yourself if you can avoid some of that negativity by adjusting your expectations of others. For example, we can tell the friend who's always late that, in the future, we're going to go ahead and eat dinner while it's still warm—with a smile, of course; we aren't threatening or reproaching, we're merely communicating our reasonable requests, ones which are intended to enhance the relationships of everyone involved. We can tell our kids that if they're not in the car when it's time to leave for school, we're going to leave and let them walk to school—hopefully, it'll only take one time for the lesson to be learned. We can let the person who betrayed our confidence know that he or she has lost our trust, and will have to earn it back.

Good communication is key to good relationships. Many of the issues that diminish or destroy our happiness can be dealt with by clearly communicating our desires to the people involved. Expecting people to know what we're thinking and feeling is unrealistic. No one can read our minds, and few people can accurately interpret mixed or unclear signals.

Notice we say to communicate to "the people involved." Never speak to someone other than the person whose actions are the cause of your angst in the hopes that it'll eventually get back to the person who you hope will change. Clear communication cannot happen "through the grapevine." Save for the unique situation of talking to a therapist or someone else who actually has the power to help, talking about others behind their backs usually doesn't work, and often makes things worse.

Take an honest look at the communication you display in your relationships. Do you clearly communicate your requests? Do you give unconditional kindness? Have you tried to do so but are dissatisfied with the results?

You *can* confront the person and his or her negative behaviors directly. When you do determine that it's time to hold someone accountable, choose the right time and place. If you enter into a serious conversation when there isn't enough time, the location isn't private, or the person is stressed or distracted, you may make the situation worse.

If you don't feel safe confronting the person directly, ask a trusted friend or advisor to join you, but be careful not to give the appearance of "ganging up" on the person.

If you are not comfortable confronting the other person, you still have options. You can distance yourself emotionally and/or physically from people who consistently let you down.

You can also try putting the situation in context with the rest of the other person's life. Is the person burdened with overwhelming responsibility? Is the person not feeling well? Is the person struggling with something you have no idea about? Did the person understand what you expected of him or her? Does the person have the IQ (intelligence quotient) or EQ (emotional quotient) to fully understand and meet your expectations? If you don't know the answers to these questions, you can give the other person the benefit of the doubt about past issues, and determine to communicate your requests more clearly in the future.

Another option is to simply lower your requirements further, or as a last resort, end the relationship and eliminate the person from your life entirely.

Regardless of how you handle situations that threaten to damage or destroy a good (or potentially good) relationship, be careful not to give anyone the power to steal your peace and happiness. By losing your peace, you give the other person far too much control over your happiness.

You must always maintain control of your peace and joy. No relationship is perfect, so there will be plenty of opportunities to practice healthy boundaries. The important thing to remember is that no matter what anyone else says or does, decide not to allow anyone or any situation to take away your peace and joy. Throughout our lives, there will be painful moments, but our suffering is optional.

The secret to good relationships is to show loving kindness without expecting anything in return. When you're able to do this, you will be happier, your relationships will improve, and you will be modeling authentic kindness for everyone within your influence. How will you improve your relationships?

Meditation

I do my best to create and maintain good relationships.

Actions

- I will value my relationships above all material things.

- I will give dignity to the people I care about by making eye contact with them and truly listening to them.

- I will bridge the gap between what I hope for from another person and where that person is at that moment by clearly communicating my expectations and modeling what I hope to see from that person in the future.

- I will praise in public and correct in private.

- I will find the good qualities of others and compliment them.

- I will be the best person I can be so that it's easy to be in a healthy relationship with me.

- I will not expect others to read my mind or know my heart. I know that to do so would be setting up unrealistic expectations, which are relationship-killers.

In all that you do, and in all that you expect of the people in your life, model the behavior you want to see in others. Then recognize and celebrate the behavior you hope to see as it happens.

On a scale of 1–10, 10 being the healthiest and most rewarding, how would you rate your relationships? How will you increase your happiness by developing and maintaining healthy relationships?

DAY 3
LAUGHTER

*"We don't laugh because we're happy—
we're happy because we laugh."*

—William James

L AUGHTER is the best medicine for whatever ails us. This is literally true. We know that laughter releases "feel good chemicals" in our brains. Laughter gives us a respite from whatever circumstances we're dealing with, lifting our spirits so that we're better equipped to handle what comes next.

Take a moment to assess the level of laughter in your life. When was the last time you laughed so hard that your stomach hurt and tears streamed down your face? If it wasn't within the last 30 days, you're not trying hard enough. We can and *should* be intentional about building laughter into our lives.

It's easier than ever now to find movies, TV shows, videos, podcasts, and live comedy at your fingertips. There are entire channels and production companies dedicated to nothing but comedy, 24/7. If you don't find yourself with reason to laugh, don't place blame on those around you; it's not anyone else's responsibility to keep your spirits uplifted.

Consistently happy people actively pursue their own happiness. This doesn't necessarily mean that they are naturally happy; in fact, some consistently happy people have a natural tendency toward depression or live with circumstances that could be depressing. These people have to deliberately fight depression. They do so by refusing to lean into sad circumstances by dwelling on them, and by trying to find the humor in even the most tense, sad, or challenging of situations.

If you truly want to be happy, decide right now that you're going to stop just pressing through, living for the next weekend, the next vacation, the next promotion, or the next goal. No one is assured of another day, so if you're only going to be happy on your days off, when you're on vacation, when you get that promotion, when you get a bigger house, when you get a newer car, etc., then you're never going to be happy. There will *always* be something more to strive for.

Make no mistake—there's nothing wrong with setting goals and striving toward your next achievement. But there is a great deal wrong with missing your opportunity to laugh *today* because the circumstances of the day don't all line up perfectly with what you hope for.

What will you do to genuinely laugh today?

Meditation

I will laugh today.

Actions

- I will find something to laugh about today and every day. I will look beyond the trials and tribulations life, and always find something humorous.

- I will seek out people who like to laugh and who tickle my funny bone.

- I will find videos that make me laugh, and keep them ready as my "go to" coping tool for times when I would rather scream or cry.

Resolve to take responsibility for your happiness today. Find something to smile about. You will enjoy your life more when you find something to laugh about.

On a scale of 1–10, 10 being highest, how would you rate your daily laughter? How will you increase your happiness by finding something to laugh about today?

DAY 4
PEACE

*"For every minute you are angry you
lose sixty seconds of happiness."*
—RALPH WALDO EMERSON

PEACE is a valuable asset that many don't even consider when thinking of their own happiness. When busyness, dysfunction, and chaos rule our lives, our stress level increases; we become less productive, and it can affect our health, our relationships, and our happiness.

If you want to be happy in life, measure, value, and guard your peace. When you lose your peace, you lose your happiness. It's that simple.

Authentic peace is internal. No one can give it to you, and no one can steal it from you, so long as you refuse to allow them to do so. Even in the midst of extreme stress and chaos, you can remain peace-filled. In fact, you can bring your peace to dysfunctional situations, and in so doing, begin to bring calm.

Imagine a cell phone dropped into a bucket of water. The phone is probably not going to work after being fully immersed; in fact, it may even be destroyed. Now imagine if the same cell phone were submerged after being sealed tightly in a plastic bag. Protected inside the bag, the cell phone remains undamaged and will continue to function despite the water surrounding it.

The same is true for us and our peace. When we develop peace within us, and guard it carefully, it will not be diminished or destroyed by external circumstances. It is important to guard our peace because of how easily it can be destroyed by ongoing stress and strife.

One way to guard your peace is to manage your expectations. Make sure that what you expect of yourself and others is reasonable. Make sure that others know, and agree to, what you expect of them. When you expect something that another person is incapable of doing or providing, you are setting yourself and the other person up for negative emotions that can diminish or destroy your peace as well as that of the other person.

An alternative to being let down is to lower your expectations to where the other person is at the moment. You wouldn't expect a baby who is just beginning to walk to run in a 10k marathon, and you wouldn't expect someone who is currently managing extreme difficulties in their life to be at their best at all times. We often make assumptions about what other people are capable of doing or how they'll behave when they may be nowhere near the level of our expectations.

This is not to suggest that we let go of our expectations for the growth and development of others. Of course we hope that others will grow and mature, but we must not allow the poor choices or behavior of others to diminish or destroy our peace.

Additionally, to keep our peace we must find a healthy balance between accepting where we are today and our hopes for where we want to be in our future.

Although we can hope for growth in ourselves and others, ultimately the only things we can truly control in this life are our own attitudes, words, actions, and feelings. When we begin to accept the truth that we cannot control others or much of what happens in this life, it becomes much easier to keep our peace.

What will you do to acquire and maintain your peace today?

Meditation

I cherish my peace, and I refuse to allow any person or situation to steal it.

Actions

- I will guard my peace today, and I will not allow anything to lead me to forfeit my peace.

- I will take a deep breath before I respond to others about anything that could lead me to lose my peace.

- I will put everything into perspective so that nothing is blown out of proportion, seeing everything for its true impact on my life.

- I will not expect more of myself or others than that which is reasonable and healthy.

As you intentionally manage your expectations of yourself and others, you will increase your peace, and the quality of your happiness and your life.

On a scale of 1–10, 10 being highest, how would you rate the level of your internal peace? How will you increase your happiness by creating peace in your life?

DAY 5
TRUST

"Happiness is not out there, it's in you."
—Anonymous

TRUST plays a huge part in our happiness. Think about how you feel when you have been betrayed. It's an awful feeling; the minute you feel as though you've been lied to, cheated on, or otherwise mistreated by someone you should have been able to trust, your happiness disintegrates.

You cannot fully control whether or not others are trustworthy. But you can intentionally seek out trustworthy people and keep them closest to you.

The best way to surround yourself with trustworthy people is to be a person who can be trusted. By being a trustworthy person, you attract others who are of the same moral fabric. By being a trusted person to everyone in your life, you build solid relationships with good people, and you model trustworthiness, which is the best way to inspire this quality in the people within your influence.

To become truly trustworthy, you must determine to be consistent—in other words, you must not say one thing while doing another. You must not criticize others for something that you, yourself, do. You must not lie about anything. You must never steal anything. You must never speak unkindly about anyone behind their back.

In other words, to become trustworthy, you must behave with integrity in every area of your life, consistent with the values you say you espouse. When you make integrity a lifestyle, eventually it will become more than second nature—it will be an inextricably inherent part of who you are.

How have you been trustworthy? What will you do in the future to show that you are trustworthy?

Meditation

I am a trustworthy person, and I seek out and build relationships with trustworthy people.

Actions

- Today, I will be someone who can be trusted with money, with information, and with the hearts of the people in my life. I will consistently maintain the same standard to which I want others to behave. Being trustworthy will model for others how to be the same way.

- From this day forward, I will have a zero-tolerance policy for deceit in any form, and I will uphold the highest of moral standards.

- I will be consistent and congruent in all areas of my life.

- I will choose the right time and place to explain to the people in my life that being able to trust others and to be trusted is very important to me, and that I have made the decision to live with integrity and to surround myself with people of integrity.

Eventually you will be surrounded with only those people who are of the same level of trustworthiness as you. When your life is filled with people whom you can count on to be honest with you, to hold what you share in confidence, and to be there for you in time of need, your happiness will be full.

On a scale of 1–10, 10 being highest, how would you rate your level of trustworthiness? How will you increase your happiness by trusting and being trusted?

DAY 6
PATIENCE

*"It's the moments that I stopped
just to be, rather than do, that have
given me true happiness."*

—RICHARD BRANSON

BEING patient can be a challenge, but as you begin to notice and value patience in yourself and others, you can train yourself and those around you to value this quality which is necessary for true happiness.

That being said, developing and valuing patience is easier said than done, because patience comes only one way—through difficult times. We don't learn powerful lessons and develop priceless character traits like patience during times of fun and ease; we learn the important character traits, like patience, only through the frustrations of life.

Authentic happiness develops after we refuse to give up, after we persevere through difficulties, and after we develop patience. It's in the "going through" that we learn the invaluable trait of patience. Having patience enhances relationships because choosing patience instead of angry outbursts says that you value the relationship more than being right or getting your way.

When the inevitable opportunity to get frustrated or angry presents itself, instead of allowing yourself to immediately slip into those emotions, take a moment and notice how you feel. Take a breath, then change the channel on your mind to something else. You can visualize a lake, a beautiful blue sky, or the rolling waves of a beach. Doing this intentionally gives you a moment to keep your peace rather than exchanging it for anger or frustration, and in so doing, you delay your response. This lapse of time allows you to intentionally develop patience.

You may still feel frustrated afterwards, despite having caught yourself from losing your patience, but hopefully the frustration will be lessened. By practicing this exercise every time you are faced with an opportunity to get frustrated or angry, you will get better and better at keeping your peace, and you will become more and more patient with yourself and with others.

Learning to gracefully navigate through the challenging experiences of life teaches us how to handle adversity, and in so doing develops patience. It's this patience we acquire as we mature and persevere through obstacles which prepares and qualifies us to successfully overcome the later challenges that we will inevitably face as we journey through life.

Consider times when you have been impatient. Think about how that made you feel. How will you become more patient from this day forward?

Meditation

I will be patient with myself and with others today.

Actions

- I understand that authentic success, and the happiness that accompanies it, will not just land in my lap one day. I will patiently wait for the things I hope for, both for myself and for others.

- When the opportunity to get frustrated, disappointed, or upset presents itself, I will choose to take a deep breath, smile, and respond calmly.

- The next time I feel like overreacting, I'm going to separate myself from the person and/or situation and give myself time to calm down before responding.

- I will give others the benefit of the doubt before reacting.

- Before I react, I will consider why others have acted, or failed to act, in ways that have disappointed, frustrated, or angered me.

- I will stay determined to be quick to forgive and slow to anger.

In a world of instant gratification, those who work on developing patience build and maintain their happiness and earn the greatest rewards.

On a scale of 1–10, 10 being highest, how would you rate your level of patience with yourself and with others? How will you increase your happiness by being patient and valuing the patience of others?

DAY 7
SELF-CONTROL

"If you aren't grateful for what you already have, what makes you think you would be happy with more?"

—ROY T. BENNETT

SELF-CONTROL is what keeps us from saying, partaking of, or doing the wrong things. Without it, we say things we cannot take back. We eat and drink too much. We buy things we don't need. And we do things we shouldn't do, all of which lead to regret, which steals our happiness. Self-control keeps us from those excesses that can lead to addiction, misery, and even tragedy.

When we self-indulge, we're comforting ourselves. We're telling ourselves that we've worked hard, or have performed well, or are weary, or that we are hurting, and we therefore deserve to have what we want, when we want it. When we live like this, we're modeling self-indulgence for everyone within our influence. This is precisely how pounds are gained, credit card balances hit their limits, and the special treats of life become mundane.

We indulge ourselves when we go out to eat, knowing that we should eat the food we've already paid for at home. In the time it takes to drive to the restaurant and wait to be seated, you could have prepared a better meal at home. We indulge ourselves when we succumb to the impulse to buy that new outfit that we weren't aware of an hour ago, yet now feel we can't live another day without. (If it's still there after you have paid all your bills and deposited into your savings account, then it was meant to be.) When we stop indulging ourselves and actually wait for the good things we want, we appreciate and enjoy them more when we finally get them.

For some of us, the indulgences that diminish our happiness are found not in ourselves, but in our family and friends. When we regularly over-indulge family or friends, we risk being taken advantage of. Rather than being grateful for the occasional extra effort, overindulgence becomes expected. This is especially true with the young people in our lives.

When we indulge children, we diminish their ability to wait for good things, and we rob them of the opportunity to learn to wait for, and to truly appreciate, rewards. Indulging young people steals the sweetness of anticipation that should be a big part of the fun of receiving something good. For many young people who are growing up in a more privileged environment than did their parents and grandparents, there are few real "treats" because what they receive on a regular basis would have been considered, just a generation prior, a treat meant only for special occasions.

Here's a challenge: Determine to go a full week without any self-indulgences. Discipline yourself. You can do it. At the end of the week, you might find that you've lost a pound and retained more of your own money. Wouldn't that make you happy?

Meditation

I will control my attitudes, words, and actions today. And I will control my appetites so that my appetites will not control me.

Actions

- I will speak and behave today in ways that are congruent with my best self.

- I will stop indulging myself by giving in to cravings. I will not allow my appetites to control me.

- I will not "treat" myself today to something that I shouldn't indulge in.

- I will not "comfort" myself with something that will not solve my problems, and may possibly make things worse.

- I will care for myself by making the short-term choices which will lead to the long-term results that will enhance my happiness.

For authentic happiness, we have to learn how to control our attitudes, words, behaviors, desires, and personal gratification.

On a scale of 1–10, 10 being highest, how would you rate your level of self-control? How will you increase your happiness by learning greater self-control?

DAY 8
PERSEVERANCE

*"When one door of happiness closes,
another opens, but often we look so long
at the closed door that we do not see the
one that has been opened for us."*
—HELEN KELLER

PERSEVERANCE is an unwillingness to give up, and is necessary for happiness by virtue of its role in achieving personal and professional success. The character trait of perseverance is what keeps you from giving up too soon—in relationships, on the job, and in your aspirations. Greater levels of happiness than we can imagine can emerge after persevering through some of the most serious challenges of our lives.

When we refuse to give up and we continue to push through, even when times get tough, we eventually experience the kind of contentment and satisfaction that cannot be attained any other way. The happiness that we experience when we've accomplished something that we (or others) didn't think we could do, or when we conquer an adversity that seemed impossible, is at a level that many will never experience.

Our natural instinct is to avoid discomfort, but this can often lead us to give up too soon, to move on to something else when the going gets tough. But successful and contented people persevere through tough times. They refuse to give up. They may step back to assess the situation and come up with a different approach, but they refuse to throw in the towel.

When we look at successful athletes, we find people who consistently put in hours of practice. When we look at successful performers, we find people who continually rehearse and hone their craft. When we look into the lives of successful business people, we often find that prior to their noteworthy success, they experienced multiple failures.

The common factor with successful people who have reached a consistently high level of happiness is their willingness and ability to look at past performances, including past failures, as data to be examined. They mine the lessons out of what they've been through, figure out what worked and what didn't, create a fresh approach, and try again. And they keep doing that until they succeed.

In the coming weeks, you will inevitably have an opportunity to give up. Don't do it! Whether it's an exercise routine, an artistic project, a book that you started to read, a class you signed up for, or any other endeavor, decide that you will, under no circumstances, give up. Press through. If your exercise routine is too difficult, make adjustments and continue rather than giving up entirely. If the book you start is boring, skim the chapter and skip ahead, but don't quit entirely. When you finish what you start, you'll feel good. When you feel good, you will be happier. In what areas will you persevere in the future?

Meditation

I will persevere through every challenge that comes my way, and I will succeed.

Actions

- From today forward, I refuse to give up.

- I will not allow challenges to overwhelm me. I will take a deep breath and calm myself.

- I will gather and analyze the information that will help me think through possible adjustments, and then I will try again.

- I will not be bullied or intimidated into quitting.

- I will do my best, and I will not compare myself to others.

After you have persevered through something minor, you'll build the confidence you need to persevere in a more difficult challenge. When you have persevered through a difficult challenge, your confidence level will increase further, along with your happiness level.

On a scale of 1–10, 10 being highest, how would you rate your level of perseverance? How will you increase your happiness by persevering through challenges?

DAY 9
GENEROSITY

"Be happy for this moment.
This moment is your life."
—OMAR KHAYYAM

GENEROSITY can be as simple as sharing your lunch, as complicated as sharing the rest of your life with another person, and as sacrificial as giving someone a kidney.

People often think of generosity as giving something they have to someone else. Acts of giving like this certainly are generous, but generosity of spirit can be even more meaningful, and can lead to the happiness of both the giver and the recipient.

Many people refrain from generosity because they think they have nothing to give—that they are barely getting by with what they have and have nothing to spare. Or, they think that what they have to offer would be meaningless to someone else.

The truth is that we all have something to give. Our "something" may be a smile, an encouraging word, or a courteous gesture like holding a door open for someone, but even the simplest kindness can make a world of difference to another person.

The most generous thing one person can give to another is time. The 24 hours we each receive every day can never be retrieved; once those hours are spent, they are gone forever. There will never be another day exactly like today. So when you spend time with someone, you are giving that person the most precious commodity you have—the time of your life. When you call a friend who is struggling, that's generosity. When you go visit a sick friend, that's generosity. When you invite someone to share a meal, that's generosity. When you take the time to smile and make eye contact with someone, you give them dignity, which is one of the most generous gifts we can give.

Let's dispense with the notion that whatever we might have to share isn't good enough or is insignificant. Sharing our kindness, our talents, our abilities, our encouraging words, our lunch, or simply ourselves by giving of our time is a necessary ingredient in the recipe for true, sustainable happiness.

Consider the times when you've been generous, and how they made you feel. How will you show your generosity today?

Meditation

I will be generous today by giving something freely to someone else without expecting anything in return.

Actions

- I will be generous today and every day by sharing what I have with others.

- I will not withhold my generosity for fear of others judging me as not good enough or not giving enough.

- I will give of my most precious asset, my time, to someone who needs an ear to listen or an encouraging word.

- When I see someone who has a need, I will do what I can to meet that need.

- When I have something that I no longer need, I will find some organization or person to give it to who can benefit from it now.

When you give up something that you no longer need, you'll find you have more space and you'll feel better about having done something good for someone else. When you share what you, yourself, need, you won't feel diminished; to the contrary, it will feel rewarding to be a generous soul. And when you can give something away that is valuable to you, you will have shifted into a lifestyle of generosity. When that happens, your happiness will be full.

On a scale of 1–10, 10 being highest, how would you rate your generosity toward others? How will you increase your happiness by being generous?

DAY 10

CONSIDERATION OF OTHERS

"The best way to cheer yourself is to try to cheer someone else up."
—MARK TWAIN

CONSIDERATION OF OTHERS is what lets us take the focus off of ourselves and our problems for a time to consider what others are going through.

Trying to discern the motivation behind a bad attitude or wrong behavior can make all the difference in a relationship. Imagine asking, "How are you feeling?" instead of "What's wrong with you?" This slight distinction shifts us from a place of blame to one of concern. Seeking to understand the underlying cause of disappointing behavior, demonstrates a level of emotional maturity that allows us to meet others where they are, giving us a greater opportunity for improving the relationship, which can lead to greater happiness for everyone involved.

Because we don't know everything that is going on with others or every hurtful thing that has happened to them, the best way we can show consideration of others is to give everyone the benefit of the doubt. Decide to take off your judge's robe, put down the gavel, and resolve to no longer judge everyone who says or does something that hurts or offends you.

There will always be people who act like jerks—who are so self-absorbed that they are oblivious to those they hurt. But most people don't fall into this category; for most people, there is something painful behind their hurtful words or actions. The rude supervisor may have just learned that his spouse is cheating on him. The co-worker who seems to be slacking off and leaving her work for others could have just learned that her child is using drugs. The clerk who appears to be ignoring you could be exhausted from caring for an ailing parent and a cranky toddler, when she's not working at her full-time job. The person who cut you off on the freeway could be rushing to get to the hospital to see her grandmother one last time.

We've all been in situations where we're not at our best. Every one of us has failed to return a greeting, has failed to include someone in an invitation, has snapped at someone, or worse. And at those times we've all hoped for grace and mercy from others. If you want to be happy, decide that from now on, instead of being hurt or angered by the words or actions of others, you're going to ask yourself, "I wonder what's wrong in his or her life."

An added benefit of being more considerate of others is that, when thinking of others, we take our minds off ourselves and our issues, which can help us to actively fight depression. Assess the times you turned your attention away from your concerns and considered the needs and wants of others. How did that make you feel?

Meditation

I will put the feelings of others before my own today.

Actions

- When someone is grouchy or irritable, I will consider what pain or fear may have led to their behavior.

- When someone insists on having his or her own way, commandeering the conversation, cutting ahead of me in line, or some other rude behavior, I will give that person the benefit of the doubt.

- I will seek to understand what others need before attending to my own needs.

- I will not judge anyone except myself.

No one gets through this life unscathed. Everyone goes through painful situations. Many of the people with whom we interact have never spoken of their painful experiences. Yet those traumas and tragedies are the lenses through which they see the world. Regardless of how well we know someone, we do not know every hurt they've experienced, or what they may be going through now. Although it may appear illogical, the truth is that when we are considerate of the feelings of others, we are ultimately happier.

On a scale of 1–10, 10 being highest, how would you rate your consideration of others? How will you increase your happiness by turning your focus from yourself to others?

DAY 11
KINDNESS

"Let no one ever come to you without leaving better and happier. Be the living expression of God's kindness: kindness in your face, kindness in your eyes, kindness in your smile."
—MOTHER TERESA

KINDNESS can spark relationships, heal brokenness, and generally make our lives better. A kind gesture can be as simple as a genuine smile given to someone who desperately needs it. Conversely, thoughtless remarks can hurt feelings, create conflict, and crush the spirits of others. Kindness can be like water on parched ground; it costs nothing, but it can mean everything.

Acts of authentic kindness speak volumes. They say, "You matter. You are worthy. You are valuable." The authentically kind person distinguishes his or herself from the crowd by developing a reputation for unconditional kindness—for acts of kindness done to others, especially those who can do nothing for them or to them.

Each one of us can develop our own unique brand of kindness by using the combined strength of our attitude, sense of humor, talents, perspective, and abilities to brighten every room that we enter. It's not difficult or costly to do, but it does involve deliberate effort.

To increase our happiness, as well as that of others, we must make the effort to notice the people around us and to deliberately smile at them. Some people need more than a smile, and while we cannot assume the responsibility of meeting every need of others, there are times when we can open a door or carry grocery bags for someone who is struggling, or share our lunch with someone who is hungry, or give an encouraging word to someone who is down.

To determine if a person needs something more than a smile, we can use our skills of observation to read the facial expressions, body language, attitudes, and words of others. This comes effortlessly to some people, and is an effort for others, but with practice, all of us can become proficient at this type of discernment.

Before you think, "This sounds like too much work—I don't have time for this," consider that simply by noticing others and by using kindness to brighten their day with an encouraging word, a funny comment, or even a smile, you increase your happiness, model kindness for everyone within your influence, and make the world a better place everywhere you go.

How "others-focused" are you? How kind are you?

Meditation

I will be kind to myself and to everyone within my influence today.

Actions

- I will be a kind-hearted person today and every day.

- I will freely give smiles to everyone I interact with today.

- I will find and mention something good about everyone with whom I interact today.

- I will leave people feeling better than when I found them.

- Before I speak, I will think about the way my words might make others feel.

- I will not raise my voice or speak critically or in anger toward anyone. Instead, I will find a way to communicate calmly and clearly in a non-threatening way.

Extending acts of kindness to everyone within your influence may, at first, feel like a tremendous effort. But once you begin to show kindness to others consistently, it'll get easier. Eventually, it will become a lifestyle, and you will have developed a reputation for being the kindest person in your family, neighborhood, workplace, and community.

On a scale of 1–10, 10 being highest, how would you rate the kindness you've shown to others? How will you increase your happiness by showing kindness?

DAY 12
LISTENING

"I think and think and think, I've thought myself out of happiness one million times, but never once into it."
—Jonathan Safran Foer

LISTENING to others more than you talk shows respect, helps you gain greater understanding of the people in your life, and will enlighten you on things you wouldn't otherwise know. Interrupting others, even to ask questions to gain clarity, is disrespectful because it commandeers control of the conversation and may cause the person to lose his or her train of thought. It's okay to ask questions, so long as we're not interrupting their conversation to do so. In fact, if we listen long enough, we'll usually hear the answer to our questions. Of course, if the other person dominates the conversation and never allows you to ask a question or make a comment, it's okay to politely excuse yourself, and leave the conversation.

Do you interrupt others while they're talking? When others are talking, are you really listening or are you considering what you'll say next? Do you tell everyone who will listen about your purchases or accomplishments? Do you enhance or exaggerate details to make yourself look better or more "important?"

Your happiness will increase exponentially when you begin to really listen to the people in your life. You'll find yourself becoming closer to people because they will feel more understood by you. Just listening to others gives them the sense that you care about them and about what concerns them.

When we listen to people talk about what they know, especially "what they know for sure," their incontrovertible truths, we expand our knowledge and understanding of them and of the world. Conversely, when we dominate conversations with what we think, know, feel, or believe, we don't learn anything new. We haven't expanded our understanding or our reach in the world.

This isn't to say that we should never share—of course we should—but our happiness increases and our lives are enhanced only when our conversations embody a respectful give-and-take of information, beliefs, and feelings.

As we begin to listen to people, we learn about different cultures, different belief systems and different areas of expertise. As we begin to open our minds in this way, it's important for us to learn how to listen without judgment. We may have vastly different beliefs and opinions, rooted in personal feelings and life experiences, but if we want to be truly happy we have to learn how to share our differing thoughts without attempting to persuade others or inferring that others are wrong or misguided in their beliefs. Even when we vehemently disagree, ultimately, we must decide to let others be who they are and to respect the beliefs and opinions that they have formed as a result of their life experiences and perspective.

We expand our world when we listen to others without feeling an obligation to persuade them of our beliefs—regardless of how strongly we believe that the other person is wrong. When we feel compelled to persist in persuading another person to our way of thinking because it will help them (think of a person trying to convince someone to quit using drugs), it helps to understand that the best way to offer advice that will be genuinely considered is through successfully building a relationship. When we really listen to others, they feel valued and understood, and we earn the right to offer our most persuasive perspectives.

How good a listener have you been?

Meditation

Today, I will listen to others without interrupting and without thinking about how I will reply. I will truly hear what others say.

Actions

- I will pause what I'm doing and make eye contact with others while they are speaking.

- I will pay attention to others when they speak to me today.

- I will not interrupt when others are speaking to me.

- I will ask any necessary clarifying questions of others so that I fully understand them before I respond.

Decide that you will listen and really hear others, and that you will resist opportunities to commandeer and dominate conversations. When you begin to listen, really listen; when you hear and understand what others are saying, you will argue less, feel less strife in your life, and your relationships will improve. You may not agree with everyone in your life, but by listening carefully, you'll have a much better understanding of why others feel as they do. In so doing, you will be modeling this excellent relationship tool for others. And the best part is, you will be happier.

On a scale of 1–10, 10 being highest, how would you rate how well you've listened to others? How will you increase your happiness by listening and really hearing others?

DAY 13
LEARNING

"Life is 10 percent what happens to you and 90 percent how you respond to it."
—Lou Holtz

LEARNING keeps your mind active and open to new ideas. It makes you a more interesting person and a more valuable colleague.

We learn in various ways: by reading, watching interesting videos, listening to others, paying attention to the actions and choices of others, and through our life experiences. In fact, when we make a conscious effort to learn something from every person with whom we interact or hear or read about, we become more well-rounded people. We learn about subjects and industries with which we have no connection. Sometimes we may only learn what not to do or how not to behave, but there is always something to learn.

In addition to traditional, formal education, we can all learn something new every day of our lives—and with the modern technology that makes online classes and endless reading and educational video watching available to all of us, this has never been more achievable.

The world is changing every day, as evidenced by the continual progression of technology. In order to keep learning and growing, it's important that we become "continuous learners." This means that in addition to learning about things that we're involved in or are interested in, we can learn about things that are outside of the areas relevant to us or that are contrary to our beliefs.

If, like many people, you find yourself only reading the same publications or listening to the same news outlets, determine to occasionally read and listen to people who represent differing points of view. Likewise, it can be invaluable to listen to people of influence in fields that are vastly different than yours. You may find that an approach to a problem in an entirely different field can provide a fresh alternative to a challenge you face.

What new things have you learned recently?

Meditation

I will learn something from everyone with whom I interact.

Actions

- I will learn something from everyone I interact with today.

- I will read something new today, even if it's a small entry in an encyclopedia or on Wikipedia.

- I will look something up today that I've always wondered about.

- I will share a new thing I've learned with someone today, and ask that person to share a new thing with me.

Regardless of how educated and experienced you are, there are always new things to learn and new areas to explore. Seek to develop a sense of wonder about the world and the people in it. The more open you are to learning new things, the greater a sense of wonder you will develop, and ultimately, the happier you will become.

On a scale of 1–10, 10 being highest, how would you rate your experience of learning new things?

How will you increase your happiness by learning something new?

DAY 14
STRENGTH

"So we shall let the reader answer this question for himself: who is the happier man, he who has braved the storm of life and lived or he who has stayed securely on shore and merely existed?"

—HUNTER S. THOMPSON

S TRENGTH is not something that we are born with. Genuine fortitude and strength of character are developed by going through the difficult times of life.

Consider the challenging, even painful, things you've gone through. With the evidence that you survived, would you say that those experiences made you resilient? Are you more resourceful than you might have otherwise been? Are you wiser? Stronger? More compassionate than the average person?

What character traits were developed by the difficult experiences of your life? Do you have a burning desire for fairness and justice because you were treated unfairly? Are you able to shift quickly from fear to action in times of crisis because of times of trouble that you successfully made it through? Are you a courageous person who runs toward a problem rather than away from it because someone once did that for you? Or because someone failed to do that for you? Are you persistent and assertive because you experienced pain as a result of someone in your life failing you or passively giving up?

Consider the weaknesses that you observe in others, whether they be characters in books or movies, or people you see on the news, or in people you know. Consider your strengths and weaknesses. Identify the areas where you are stronger than others. Have you made it through a serious illness? Have you survived trauma? Have you persevered through a difficult situation? In every one of those areas, you are probably stronger than you give yourself credit for.

Take a look at your personality and the way you cope with stress. Do you adapt to different people and cultures because you were moved around a lot as a kid? Are you conscientious and hard-working because you strived to please someone who was "un-pleasable?" Do you work at being positive and optimistic because you have been surrounded by negative, depressed people?

For all you've been through, you're still alive, you're still in the game, and with your strength of character your best days are still ahead of you! Give yourself credit for your strength, resilience, and other good character traits, and for your learned abilities, and healthy coping skills that you developed to survive the difficult times of your life, and you will feel better about yourself and more empowered, and consequently, you will be happier.

What good came of your experiences, or what good could come of them? How has your strength benefitted you and others?

Meditation

I am stronger because of—not in spite of—the difficulties I have survived.

Actions

- I am stronger than I used to think I was.

- I may get knocked down, but I will always get up.

- It's okay to have areas of weakness because I have strengths in other areas.

- I'm wiser and more resilient because of what I've been through.

There is an old saying: "What doesn't kill you makes you stronger." Give yourself credit for surviving all you've been through. Accept that you cannot change the past, and determine to be a better person because of what you've been through.

On a scale of 1–10, 10 being highest, how would you rate your personal strength? How will you increase your happiness by valuing and using your strength?

DAY 15
COURAGE

"My mission in life is not merely to survive, but to thrive; and to do so with some passion, some compassion, some humor, and some style."
—MAYA ANGELOU

COURAGE isn't just for our military, police officers, fire fighters, and emergency medical professionals. Courage is something that each of us can develop to deal with the unavoidable stresses of life. It takes courage to confront a loved one who is making poor choices. It takes courage to date again after a bad break-up. It takes courage to go on that ninth job interview after losing your job.

Courage is that quality of mind that enables a person to face difficulty, danger, and the possibility of pain. Courage is a character trait that isn't much talked about these days. We often fail to recognize and celebrate courage, but without courage, we can never experience the fullness of the potential happiness that is possible for us.

No good relationship will blossom without our first having the courage to make ourselves vulnerable. No great difficulty can be overcome without the courage to keep trying. No new invention will ever become a reality without the courage to keep striving. No new company will ever be started without the courage to take calculated risks. No new social movement will ever help anyone without someone first having the courage to launch it.

Consider the times you've shown courage. Give yourself credit for the times that, as a young child, you walked into a classroom for the first time; the times when you applied for a job or walked in for a job interview; and the times when you asked someone out for the first time. All of these actions took courage, and without having mustered the courage to do what you've done, you wouldn't have experienced the satisfaction and joy of having accomplished and achieved those things that have enriched your life.

When you begin to recognize and celebrate courage, you'll find that you're more willing to step out of your comfort zone to try new things. To develop more courage, consider those things that you fear—those things that may be holding you back. Ask yourself what might happen if you use your courage to take a step toward doing the things you fear. You'll be no worse off if you try and fail, but you may find that you're much better off for having tried. How will you show courage in the future?

Meditation

I will face today, and everything that comes with it, with courage.

Actions

- I will face whatever happens today with the courage to see it through while doing my best.

- When I feel fear, I will remind myself of other times that I summoned the courage to press through.

- If I am faced with an overwhelming situation, I will think of other people who have courageously made it through, and I will draw inspiration from their courage.

You have made it this far, and whether you recall being courageous in the past or not, you have been! You are likely more courageous than you give yourself credit for. Some days, it takes courage just to get out of bed. You've gotten through tough times in the past, and your courage will see you through in the future.

On a scale of 1–10, 10 being highest, how would you rate your courage? How will you increase your happiness by using your courage and valuing the courage of others?

DAY 16
HONESTY

"Plenty of people miss their share of happiness, not because they never found it, but because they didn't stop to enjoy it."

—William Feather

HONESTY and the related quality of sincerity are foundational to happiness. Honesty builds a good reputation for us and helps us avoid the drama and conflict that result from deceit.

Candidly consider the times in the past when you were dishonest or insincere. How does that make you feel?

There are several reasons that people are dishonest. Oftentimes, it's because they think they would be embarrassed by the truth—they are afraid of what people would think of them if they knew the truth about them. One of the fastest ways to eliminate that type of dishonesty from your life is to decide to own your story. That means choosing to be—and accept—your delightfully flawed self.

Most people waste the priceless time they're granted in this life trying to be acceptable, to fit in. Rather than value their own unique combination of assets, many people aspire to be like someone else. Actors want to be "the next Tom Cruise," performers want to be the next "Beyoncé," authors strive to be "the next J.K. Rowling," and millions of followers want to be like the Kardashians. There is nothing wrong with aspiring to greatness, so long as you pursue your own unique brand of greatness.

You have something that all those famous people and all those "wannabes" don't have. You may not know what it is yet; sadly, lots of people live most of the years of their lives without knowing what it is. The good news is that if you don't yet know, you can discover it. If you know it, you can hone it. And once you do that, you will have everything you need to fulfill the purpose for which you were born, and to enjoy all that accompanies it, including authentic happiness.

So what is it that you have that the celebrities, athletes, and success icons don't have? Your story—and the lessons you've mined from it. You are the world's foremost expert on YOU and your story. You are the world's foremost expert on the experiences you've lived through and the lessons you've learned as a result of those experiences—especially the painful experiences that you successfully survived.

The secret to happiness is deciding to never again be ashamed of yourself or of what you've been through, what was done to you, what you've done, or any of the other experiences of your past. That was yesterday. This is today. Let go of the hurt, the shame, the regret, and the coulda, shoulda, woulda's.

When you decide to own what you've been through, it no longer has any control over you. And when you mine the good character traits, learned abilities, and coping skills that were developed through those events, you are virtually mining the nuggets of gold out of those experiences. Keep the gold and toss the trash. Refuse to keep any negative feelings, like anger or shame.

Those feelings may be associated with your past, but they have no place in your future.

Once you've done that, you can use these newly discovered assets, and the candid honesty that accompanies them, to create personal and professional success. Real success, accompanied by authentic happiness, is truly the best response to adverse experiences.

Once you've made the decision to be you and to own your own story—your words, actions, and attitudes—it's important to refrain from doing or saying anything that is inconsistent with the person you want to be. So long as you do that, you will have nothing to lie about!

Own your story, be your honest, transparent, awesome self, and you will be happier than you have ever thought possible.

Think about a time when you weren't completely honest. How does that make you feel?

Meditation

I will be honest today, and I will refuse every temptation to engage in deceit in any form.

Actions

- I will not lie about anything today.

- There is no need for me to exaggerate—I am good enough.

- I will be sincere and genuine, even if I have to say something that won't be received well.

- I will not be insincere in order to fit in or to falsely compliment someone. The truth is always best, even when it isn't well received.

You are good enough—in fact, you are awesome! You have a unique set of strengths, talents, learned abilities, experiences, and perspectives that were formed through your life experiences, which are authentically yours. When you stop trying to appear perfect and quit striving to be accepted, you will discover that you are the most awesome version of you that has ever walked the Earth. This new, healthy perspective on your worth and value will open the door to a level of honesty, sincerity, and happiness that you never thought possible, because when you accept yourself, you no longer have to compete with others or worry about what others think of you.

On a scale of 1–10, 10 being highest, how would you rate your honesty about yourself and your circumstances? How will you increase your happiness by maintaining uncompromising honesty?

DAY 17

POSITIVE ATTITUDE

*"Most folks are as happy as they
make up their minds to be."*
—ABRAHAM LINCOLN

A **POSITIVE ATTITUDE** is one of the most powerful factors in your happiness and one of the most influential aspects of your life. It is more important than your home, your car, or having food in your pantry—because with a positive attitude, you can get all those other things.

One of the key things necessary to maintaining a positive attitude is to stop yourself from getting easily offended. Decide right now that you will refuse to allow yourself to feel hurt or angry because of what someone else says or does. You may think that you have no control over feelings of hurt, frustration, disappointment, or anger, but you have more control than you realize. You may not be able to control the feelings as they come, but your response to those feelings will control how long they stay, and how much influence they will have over you. The minute you take offense, you have allowed the person who offended you to kill your positive attitude. In other words, you can have hurt and angry feelings, or you can have a positive attitude, but you cannot have both.

Until you learn this critical lesson, you will not have consistent happiness. You will live your life subject to the ups and downs that result from the comments and actions of others. You will have given control of your attitude over to others, to be manipulated as easily as a puppet dangling from its strings.

Only the most trusted of people should have access to the strings that control your emotions. When you give someone the power to make you feel content, you also give that person the power to make you feel hurt. That's why it's important to avoid making your self-esteem contingent on the approval of others, because when you do that, your self-esteem will tank when that approval is withdrawn. So how do you avoid having your self-esteem damaged by others? Answer: By valuing your awesome self and guarding your positive attitude.

Consider how you felt at times in the past when, for whatever reason, you had a negative attitude. Now think of times when you've had a positive attitude. Do you recall how that felt? Do you see how maintaining a positive attitude will contribute to your happiness?

Meditation

I choose to have a positive attitude today. I choose to believe that, no matter what happens, everything will work out beautifully.

Actions

- I will adopt and maintain a positive attitude.

- I will choose to be positive by looking for the upside in every situation.

- I will believe the best of others.

- I will actively fight depression by thinking of something that makes me smile or laugh.

- I will picture negative thoughts like a big beach ball. When they fly my way, I will simply push them away. I will not embrace the negative thought. If I am already holding a negative thought, I will get rid of it.

- I will be content with what I think of my awesome self rather than allowing my positive attitude to be diminished by what others may or may not think of me.

- I will learn to think of my feelings as puppet strings. One string is "hurt," another is "anger," still another is "envy." I refuse to give anyone the power to yank my strings!

Consistently maintaining a positive attitude can be an enormous undertaking, but it can be done. And the sooner you decide to do it, the better off you'll be. Remember:

Eliminating negativity = improved positivity = more happiness.

On a scale of 1–10, 10 being highest, how would you rate your positivity? How will you increase your happiness by choosing to have a positive attitude?

ORGANIZATION

"Happiness is about learning how to cultivate the mindset and behaviors that have been empirically proven to fuel greater success and fulfillment."

—SHAWN ACHOR

ORGANIZATION can enhance our peace and help make us successful.

What's the opposite of organization? Answer: chaos. We've all experienced the rush of adrenaline that accompanies the realization that we've lost our phone, or the fear that we're going to be late because we can't find our car keys, or the sense of dread that creeps up on us when we can't find our car in a large parking lot.

Disorganization, and the dysfunction that it brings, can steal our happiness and diminish our ability to achieve our goals and fulfill our purpose. On the other hand, when our schedules, living spaces, and work spaces are organized, we are more peaceful, more efficient, and far more productive.

There are many things in life that we cannot control, like the attitudes and actions of others, and the crises that can interrupt our lives through no fault of our own, but we have a great deal of control over our own personal level of organization.

This is true even for those of us who are not naturally organized. If you are not as organized as you would like to be, read a book or watch a video on how to get organized. Listen to others who have transformed their lives by purging the unnecessary items and activities that drain their energy and attention, and then begin your own journey toward organization.

Sometimes, our lack of organization is a result of having failed to pay attention to what we were doing—where we put down our keys, when we absently nodded in agreement to do something, or when we were trying to do several things at once. A big part of a lack of organization is the fact that we are not fully focused on the here and now.

With all the things that compete for our attention, it's no wonder that we tend toward disorganization. In addition to the personal interactions with the people we live and work with, there are phone calls, texts, emails, social media notifications, the 24/7 news cycle, and the circumstances of life that we have to navigate through on a daily basis. In order to remember something, we have to first be mindful of it. Our level of organization will always be in direct relation to how truly present and mindful we are in our lives.

The good news is that there are some simple things that you can do to become more mindful and present. For example, you can create a set schedule for your daily tasks, and stay on that schedule (except for urgent emergencies). To avoid interruption to your thoughts and tasks, you can turn off notifications on your electronics, or check and respond at set times throughout the day. Meditation and prayer can be helpful. Taking a "mindful moment" several times throughout your day to simply quiet your mind and breathe can help you be more mindful of yourself, your surroundings, and your circumstances.

You can also develop routines and compensatory skills that will help you to always find your keys (because they will consistently be in the same place); to avoid preventable social faux pas, like forgetting an important birthday (because your calendar is up-to-date); to prevent "surprise" expenses like car registrations and insurance premiums that sneak up on you (despite the fact that these same things snuck up on you 365 days ago); and so on.

During these 30 days, if you invest in learning and implementing organizational techniques, you will find that you will have eliminated some of the chaos, dysfunction, unnecessary expense, anxiety, and hurt feelings that can result from living a disorganized life. The best part is that when you eliminate the problems that result from lack of organization, you will have more time to do the things you want to do, which lead to increased happiness.

Consider the times when you have been late because you couldn't find your keys or when you couldn't find the important papers you needed for an appointment. Recall how that made you feel. Now consider how in control, in charge, and peaceful you will feel when everything is in its proper place, and you know right where it is.

Meditation

I will invest the time needed to become more organized, because organization will help me feel more in control and happier.

Actions

- I will be mindful and fully present today.

- I will be aware of my words, actions, and surroundings so that, in the future, I will remember what I've done, what I've agreed to do, and where I have put things.

- I will be organized in my thinking and my actions today. I determine to do one thing until it's done. If I have to set something aside for a time, I will make a note about what I have to do so that I will be prompted to complete what I started.

- I will develop a system of organization that works for me.

People who are organized are more likely to be prepared to take advantage of opportunities that arise—opportunities which can lead to a greater sense of fulfillment, contentment, and happiness than you may be able to imagine. So, do yourself a favor: assess your level of organization and take steps to get more organized in every area of your life.

On a scale of 1–10, 10 being highest, how would you rate your organization? How will you increase your happiness by getting more organized?

DAY 19
FRUGALITY

"Success is getting what you want.
Happiness is wanting what you get."
—DALE CARNEGIE

FRUGALITY is valuable regardless of how much money you earn. Being cautious with your money in the short-term will lead to happiness in the long-term, because you'll have the money you need for any unexpected situations that arise, or the money you want for the things that can enhance your happiness. For example, frugal people are able to avoid potential train wrecks of unhappiness by not purchasing things on credit that they are not confident they can pay for.

Some people confuse frugality with being "cheap," but the truth is that there is an important distinction between the two. Being frugal is about managing your money, regardless of how much or how little you have. It means that you have the wisdom to postpone self-gratification until a time when you can better afford the thing you want to purchase or until a time when the item can be obtained at a better price. The best way to learn to become frugal is to learn to delay purchases. The best way to do that is to begin to make financial decisions based on facts rather than emotions.

Being cheap is synonymous with stingy. It is the opposite of generous. A cheap person may spend large sums of money, but only for his or her own self-gratification. A cheap person may make emotional, rather than fact-based, decisions about money, and in so doing may make foolish decisions, like buying things on impulse or at a lower quality than was available elsewhere, had they taken the time to shop and consider all their options. Being cheap doesn't necessarily imply a character flaw. People who are cheap may be so because of childhood messages, cultural influences, or familial patterns.

Being frugal does not mean being stingy. In fact, the opposite is often true: people who are frugal can be extremely generous because they are careful with their money, and consequently have money to spend on others or to donate to charity.

Being frugal indicates a level of responsibility and good stewardship with whatever level of resources the person has. Being frugal can be a very desirable trait to an employer or business partner because a frugal person can be trusted not to make foolish and costly business decisions.

Frugality can be adopted by anyone at any time. Of course, it can be especially helpful for people who lack sufficient financial provision. Regardless of our level of financial prosperity (or lack thereof), we can all improve our money management skills. We can all improve our ability to shop for the best price, or to negotiate a better price, before making our purchases. And we can all improve our ability to delay our gratification, and thus enjoy our purchases more when we do make them.

Consider times when you have spent money foolishly. Recall how it made you feel to have

exchanged your money for something that is now worthless. How will you feel when you have money saved up because of your choice to be frugal?

Meditation

I will be frugal today by not spending money on things I don't need.

Actions

- Today, I will take an honest look at the money that I spend.

- I will take the time to consider what I really want, and to compare price and quality before making a purchase.

- I will spend money on things that help me succeed in life and not on things that will be worthless before they're fully paid for.

- I will spend money on things that enhance my happiness and the quality of my life.

Learning how to manage what we've earned or been given is important to our happiness, because we all know that unhappiness can accompany a lack of something. When we are frugal, we enjoy what we have and we have what we enjoy. When we are frugal, we exercise greater wisdom regarding money. We no longer make emotional decisions about money. Rather, we make fact-based financial decisions, and thus diminish emotional ties to material things, which naturally leads to greater happiness.

On a scale of 1–10, 10 being highest, how would you rate your frugality? How will you increase your happiness by being more frugal?

DAY 20
HUMILITY

*"It isn't what you have or who you are
or where you are or what you are doing
that makes you happy or unhappy.
It is what you think about it."*
—DALE CARNEGIE

HUMILITY is a precursor for greatness. The opposite, arrogance, is often a precursor for embarrassment.

Humble people do not demand that things go their way. Humble people feel no need to tell others about accomplishments, purchases, travel, etc. Humble people know that they are far more valuable than their title at work, the degrees they hold, or the accolades they've achieved. They know that the content of their character is to be valued above whatever money they have earned, the house they live in, or the car they drive.

Because humble people understand and value humility, they tend to recognize it in others. They emphasize the importance of it to those closest to them, often more through actions than words. Humble people don't fight for control of the conversation because they have no need to prove superiority to others. They listen more than they talk, and consequently, learn much from others.

Conversely, arrogant people seize every opportunity to tell anyone who will listen about their latest conquest or acquisition. They thrive on making sure that everyone within earshot knows how important they are or how knowledgeable they are. These are the people who "name drop" in an effort to build their importance in the eyes of others. They interrupt others and dominate the conversation, including those conversations about topics on which they are not experts. What arrogant people don't understand is that with every comment they make or story they tell they reveal more of their insecurities and faults.

We can see clearly why humble people are often offered opportunities that would never be extended to their arrogant counterparts. Humble people will rarely embarrass their family, friends, or employers by their words or actions. They will often be the ones to help others avoid public embarrassment because they have no need to elevate themselves by demeaning someone else. They rise to greatness in their fields of endeavor because when they do speak up, they are knowledgeable and well-prepared.

Consider times when others thought you were a "know-it-all." Can you imagine the respect you will garner when you develop a reputation for being humble and respectful?

Meditation

I will be humble today, and will not think more highly of myself than others.

Actions

- Of the seven billion people on earth, I do not believe I'm the smartest or the best. I will be humble today.

- I will not demand my own way today.

- I will not argue with anyone to prove that I'm right.

- I will not impose my opinions or my will on anyone today.

As you think about the times when you've been less than humble, consider how it makes you feel. Determine to not make conversations about you. Hold back in offering your opinions, perspectives, or stories until you are asked to share, and then take notice how good these moments of humility make you feel.

On a scale of 1–10, 10 being highest, how would you rate your humility? How will you increase your happiness by being more humble?

DAY 21

BE A GOOD EXAMPLE

"The happiness of your life depends upon the quality of your thoughts."
—MARCUS AURELIUS

BEING A GOOD EXAMPLE is the best way to change the world!

It's also the best way to create a legacy. When you live your life as though everyone was watching, you are literally modeling right living for others. You inspire others, especially young people, to rise up and do the right thing—to make better choices and to treat others better. Living right and being a good example is far more powerful than preaching, admonishing, or scolding others.

Being a good example means not asking someone to pick up a ringing phone and tell whoever's on the other end that you're not there. It means not cutting corners on your tax return. It means not breaking laws—and that includes speed limits. It means treating others with respect, even when they don't deserve it. It means showing mercy to people who are having hard times, giving grace to people who aren't behaving their best, and forgiving and letting go of intentionally inflicted wounds.

Treating others well and making right choices is the best possible decision you can make because the beauty of living well is that good will come back to you. The adage "What goes around, comes around" is true. When you treat others well, you will be treated well (though maybe not by same people). When you make good choices, you will get good results. And when you enjoy the results of those good choices, it motivates you to do even better.

Whether you're trying or not, you are an example (for good or bad) to everyone within your influence. If you do wrong, you're literally saying to others in your life, "It's okay for you to do this, too." If you do good, you're saying to others, "It's worth the effort to do this."

Where have you been a good example to others? Where have you blown it? Be honest.

Meditation

I will be a good example of how to treat people well and make right choices.

Actions

- I will make right choices today, even when no one is looking.

- I will treat people the way I would like to be treated.

- I will do my best to be a good example in everything I do and say—in my facial expressions, body language, and attitude.

- I will set an example with what I consume today, including what I listen to, what I watch, what I eat, and what I purchase. I know that every action sets an example for others to follow.

Consider the examples you set in every area of your life. Are you a good example in your home? In your neighborhood? In your community? At work? At play? It's important to set a good example in all aspects of your life. We are only happy to the extent that we make right choices and treat people well, from our closest family and friends, to extended family, to neighbors, co-workers, and everyone else.

On a scale of 1–10, 10 being highest, how would you rate the example you set? How will you increase your happiness by being a good example?

DAY 22
RELIABILITY

"Now and then it's good to pause in our pursuit of happiness and just be happy."
—GUILLAUME APOLLINAIRE

RELIABILITY is the trait of always doing what you say you're going to do. It means being consistent and congruent; in other words, having your words match your actions.

Conversely, people who say one thing but do something entirely different are unreliable. You would never ask an unreliable person to get you to the airport on time, or take care of your children, or to be responsible for getting you to work for your first day on the job. In the same way, good jobs and exciting opportunities are rarely offered to unreliable people. Dependable, consistent people rarely seek out unreliable people as employees, business partners, friends or spouses.

Reliable people tend to attract good people and good opportunities into their lives. They can be depended upon to do what they say they're going to do. And if ever an otherwise-reliable person does let you down, you can be assured that something serious is going on in his or her life.

Reliable people are there when you need them most. They don't abandon you when you go through tough times. These are the people who show up with chicken soup when you don't feel well or who pick you up from the side of the road when your car breaks down. If you have these people in your life, recognize and celebrate this excellent trait in them. If you are a reliable person, give yourself credit for being so. If you have not been terribly reliable in the past, determine to do better from this day forward.

If you want to have reliable people in your life, you must be a reliable person. Take stock of your level of reliability. Ask yourself: how dependable am I as a family member? As a friend, or as a neighbor, or as a co-worker or employee? Do you agree to do things that you don't really intend to do and then cancel at the last minute? Do you agree to go somewhere with someone and then change your mind when the time comes? Or worse, have you ever said you would be somewhere and then just not shown up?

If you've ever committed to do something that you didn't follow through with, don't be too hard on yourself. We've all done it at one time or another. Things come up; life happens. What matters is your determination to be reliable in the future. From this day forward, determine to develop a reputation for being reliable.

Before committing to go somewhere or to do something, ask yourself if you would agree to the request if it was within the hour. Literally think through whether or not you'd want to make that effort right now. If the answer is no, politely decline. Don't agree just because you think the other person will dislike you or be disappointed with you. He or she will be more upset if you agree and then fail to follow through. And you will be unhappy if you spend the irreplaceable time of your life doing something that you never really wanted to do in the first place.

Don't allow yourself to be pressured into something you aren't comfortable doing. Don't overcommit yourself to people who demand more from you than you can give. And don't do things you don't want to do in order to earn the respect, approval, or friendship of someone else, because whatever you do to get them to like you is what you'll have to do to keep them liking you. You're awesome already; you don't need anyone else's acceptance or approval to prove that!

Can you recall a time when someone has been unreliable and has let you down? Can you recall a time when you did that to someone else? How does that make you feel?

Meditation

Today, I will do everything I say I will do, to the best of my ability.

Actions

- I will not agree to do something unless I am confident that I will be able to do it. My yes means yes, and my no means no.

- I will not be pressured into agreeing to do something that is in conflict with my values or which I strongly do not want to do.

- Today, my words and actions will be congruent. I will not say one thing but do something different.

- I will model reliability and dependability for everyone within my influence.

Simply do what you say you will do, and mean what you say. Period. When you do this, you can reasonably expect reliability from others. You, as well as the other reliable people in your life, will be happier as a result.

On a scale of 1–10, 10 being highest, how would you rate your reliability? How can you increase your happiness by improving your reliability?

DAY 23
SELF-RESPECT

"People wait all week for Friday, all year for summer, all life for happiness. Stop waiting and choose happiness."

—ANONYMOUS

SELF-RESPECT is valuing yourself—knowing that you are enough, that you don't have to compete with anyone, that you are the world's foremost expert on you and the perspective formed by your life experiences. Self-respect means not having to compete with anyone else. It means valuing yourself enough to keep what is intimately yours to yourself. This includes your most private thoughts, aspirations, feelings, and actions.

If you want to be happy, quit comparing yourself to others and competing with others. You'll never be that other person—nor should you want to be. You were not built for anyone else's life. There is a good plan for your life, one for which you were perfectly created and matched. Competing with others is a waste of time that will not result in the happiness you seek and the good life you deserve. In fact, trying to be like others will distract you from becoming your best self.

Deciding not to compare yourself to or to compete with others is easier said than done. In our culture, you can be judged as a winner or a loser depending on how many social media followers you have and how many likes you get, for the kind of shoes you wear, the kind of car you drive, the zip code you live in, and on and on.

The real question is, " Who's the judge?" Who are these judges who decide who the winners and losers will be in that moment? What are their qualifications to judge us? Are they winners themselves, in every area of their lives? And even when you are declared the winner, how long until someone else knocks you out of the winner's circle? Should we be giving anyone, especially an anonymous judge, any control over our self-esteem and our lives?

Here's the truth: no one is qualified to judge you. The dirty little secret is that most people who judge do so because they're not winners, and they don't want anyone else to be a winner, either. By labeling others as losers, they hold them down. These "cool people," the self-appointed judges, elevate themselves by putting other people down. The pressure they feel to succeed is lessened if others aren't excelling beyond them and leaving them behind.

By caring about and striving for the ridiculous things by which others measure us, we give far too much control over to these people, often people we don't even know, who do not deserve the right to put us down. Your happiness should not be determined by whether or not you have the "right" kind of sneakers, the designer handbag, the fancy car, or the house with a view. Your happiness should not be affected one way or the other by how many people like your social media posts, or if they invite you to join their group (or don't), or if they say anything good (or bad) about you. If you give people control to make you happy, they can use that control to make you unhappy. No one should have that kind of control over your happiness.

Of course, it's nice when people understand us, value us, invite us, and compliment us. It feels good. But we have to decide to be happy regardless of whether or not we have all these things. The control switch for our happiness should be inside of us, rather than outside for anyone to walk up and flip on or off. Have the self-respect to pull your happiness control switch inside, and guard it with your life.

Quit measuring your happiness by the arbitrary decisions of anonymous judges. Don't let other people's opinions of what's good or bad, or in or out of style, affect your happiness one way or the other. Even if you do strive to achieve the approval of others, all that will happen is a brief reign at the top, before the rules change, and your status plummets. Someone else will be the new winner, and you'll be yesterday's news.

Ask yourself honestly if you have respected yourself in the past year? Or have you given yourself away to people who didn't deserve the most precious gifts you can give—your friendship, your confidence, your intimacy, or the time of your life that you can never get back?

Meditation

I am enough.

Actions

- I will respect myself today by taking care of myself.

- I will respect myself today by making right choices.

- I will respect myself today by valuing my delightfully awesome self—flaws and all.

- I will not allow anyone else's opinions of me to influence my happiness.

Have the self-respect to be you. Get off the happiness roller coaster of competition and be happy with who you are and what you have, beginning with your good character traits, talents, learned abilities, attitude, and so much more.

On a scale of 1–10, 10 being highest, how would you rate your level of self-respect? How will you increase your happiness by respecting yourself?

DAY 24
FAITH

"Attitude is a choice. Happiness is a choice. Optimism is a choice. Kindness is a choice. Giving is a choice. Respect is a choice. Whatever choice you make makes you. Choose wisely."
—ROY T. BENNETT

FAITH in something bigger than ourselves brings immeasurable benefit. It gives you hope, offers opportunities to broaden your perspective beyond yourself, and expands your thinking beyond your current understanding. People who choose to have faith in something have a life-preserver, something they can hold onto through the toughest experiences of their life.

Everyone experiences pain. No one gets through this life entirely unscathed. In light of this, you can go through life without faith in something bigger than yourself, or you can choose to believe that there is something greater. The simple truth is that you'll be happier if you choose to have faith.

The challenge is that we must choose to have faith. Take faith in God as an example: there is no known scientific way of proving God's existence, or of verifying whether our perceptions of God are accurate. If there was a way of proving the existence of God, no faith would be required. It is in choosing faith that we gain hope, and hope is integral to happiness.

Regardless of where you fall on the faith spectrum, there will come a time in your life when faith can help you. The powerful belief that your life matters, and that there is a good purpose for your life that you are uniquely qualified to fulfill, will become one of your greatest gifts.

If applicable, reevaluate any childhood messages you may still be carrying regarding faith. Perhaps family members pressured you to accept their religious beliefs; perhaps you perceived that being part of a specific faith group made you more or less "cool." Working from your more mature perspective, decide which childhood messages you will choose to keep and which you will leave behind.

Once you have sorted through your childhood messages, decide to be open to giving your own personal faith an opportunity to develop. The best and easiest way to begin to build your faith is to say a prayer and then to pay attention to what happens next. How will you choose faith or deepen your faith?

Meditation

Today, I choose to have faith.

Actions

- Faith is a choice, and today I choose to have faith.

- Today I will pray for the blessings of faith, hope, and love.

- Today I will eschew any negative messages through which I have filtered the notion of faith, and I will open my mind and heart to something greater than myself.

People who have a strong sense of faith report being better able to navigate through the challenges of life with more peace and less anxiety, and consequently, experience greater happiness. Determine to increase your happiness by building your faith.

On a scale of 1–10, 10 being highest, how would you rate your faith? How will you increase your happiness by choosing to have faith?

DAY 25
COOPERATION

"They say a person needs just three things to be truly happy in this world: someone to love, something to do, and something to hope for."
—TOM BODETT

COOPERATION means setting aside differences to work together toward a common goal. Cooperation helps move everyone toward success. Lack of cooperation, by contrast, halts progress and holds everyone back, leading to the diminished happiness of everyone involved.

One way to improve your level of cooperation is to decide today to stop putting labels on yourself and others. Whether we acknowledge it or not, we are less willing to cooperate with people who we think of as different than ourselves, people who believe differently, or act differently, or are from a different group. We tend to be more willing to go along with and cooperate with those who we feel share our beliefs, thoughts, and values.

There are a virtually unlimited number of variables with which we have come to distinguish ourselves from others or used to align ourselves with others. Labels create separation, and separation diminishes relationships. When we label ourselves by the color of our skin, our gender, our hair color, political affiliation, highest educational level achieved, our faith (or lack thereof), job title, zip code, or even as survivors of trauma or disease, we run the risk of diminishing our ability to respect each other and to cooperate with one another.

It can be convenient and, in some cases, necessary to label ourselves. It can be helpful to provide medical professionals with identifiers that they need to make recommendations about medications and treatment. We need identifiers on our driver's licenses to prove our identities and to obtain professional licenses and the like.

But beyond that, labels do more harm by separating us than good by uniting us. Try walking into a room full of people you don't know and announce that you are a conservative Republican or a liberal Democrat. You will immediately see the dividing lines being drawn, while the opportunity for real cooperation is immeasurably diminished.

Many labels aren't as obviously divisive as politics, religion, or nationality, but regardless of the label, they all have the potential to shut down conversation and superimpose stereotypes. When we use labels, we are effectively announcing the filter through which we see the world, the consequence of which is that people who see things differently and who wish to avoid conflict choose to keep their thoughts and opinions to themselves. When that happens, we miss out on opportunities to learn about and from each other.

When we talk to people who think, feel, and believe differently than we do, we learn who they are and why they think and feel the ways they do. Although we may not agree, we gain a better understanding of the other person, as well as a different perspective.

How have you been cooperative? How have you hindered cooperation in the past?

Meditation

I will identify new opportunities to be cooperative today, and pursue them to the best of my ability.

Actions

- I will adopt an attitude of cooperation today and every day.

- I will choose to believe that cooperation and collaboration will earn greater results than would demanding my way.

- I will try to find something that I can agree on rather than focusing on differences.

- I am willing to try to understand why others feel the way they do.

- I will not judge or criticize others for feeling differently than I do.

We can learn to respect the opinions and beliefs of others without agreeing with them or trying to persuade them to share our views. Some of the most rewarding relationships and highest levels of cooperation and the results thereof, can be found between people who disable their labels and just share honestly without fear of judgement or criticism. To the extent that we can disagree without demeaning or demonizing others, we'll all be happier.

On a scale of 1–10, 10 being highest, how would you rate your level of cooperation with others, especially those who are in some way different from you? How will you increase your happiness by cooperating and collaborating more with others?

DAY 26
FORGIVENESS

"Happiness, not in another place but this place . . . not for another hour, but this hour."
—WALT WHITMAN

FORGIVENESS releases the toxins in our hearts and cleanses the pipeline through which happiness flows. Forgiving people who have hurt us is one of the most difficult things we can do, but it's one of the most important to our long-term happiness.

The very core of forgiveness is that it is given to people who do not deserve it. What's commonly misunderstood is that forgiveness isn't for the other person—it's actually for us. The people who hurt us are still subject to the consequences of their actions, but the act of forgiveness means that we're choosing not to be hurt by them or by their actions any longer. Every moment that we refuse to forgive is a moment that we give over to the people and circumstances that have harmed us. You can stop the pain by refusing to give one more moment of your life.

Harboring bitterness or resentment toward someone saps your happiness and holds you back from living your best life. Holding onto grudges is like taking a sip of poison every day: eventually, it kills you. Imagine dying from the effects of that poison, all the while knowing that the person who hurt you will go on to live his or her life without missing a beat. Don't give anyone the satisfaction of knowing that you're still suffering over what they've done to you or failed to do for you.

Ask yourself if you have truly and fully forgiven the people who have hurt you, or if you are still carrying around those toxic feelings of anger and resentment. While you're at it, ask if you have forgiven yourself for your poor choices, angry words, or past bad behavior. If so, forgive yourself today and stop living with guilt and regret.

Consider how these negative emotions make you feel. How will you increase your happiness by leaving toxic feelings in your past where they belong?

Meditation

I will forgive those who hurt me. I will not allow unforgiveness, bitterness, or resentment to steal my happiness.

Actions

- I will forgive everyone who has harmed me, intentionally or unintentionally. I refuse to harbor the poison of bitterness or resentment one more day.

- I will forgive myself for everything I've ever done, said, or thought that was not in alignment with my best self.

- I will forgive myself for the times that I failed to do or say the things that I should have done or said.

- I will release any and all feelings of regret, unforgiveness, bitterness, or resentment.

If you owe someone an apology, give it. If someone owes you an apology, forgive them, whether they apologize or not. Remember: authentic forgiveness is always undeserved. If someone hurt you or shamed you, don't give that person the power to hurt or shame you for one moment longer. Once you've done this, forgive yourself for any regrets you're holding onto. Start fresh today with a clean slate, determined to live a life of happiness unhindered by negativity.

On a scale of 1–10, 10 being highest, how would you rate your forgiveness? How will you increase your happiness through forgiveness?

DAY 27
CREATIVITY

*"Happiness lies in the joy of achievement
and the thrill of creative effort."*
—FRANKLIN D. ROOSEVELT

CREATIVITY is the way we best express our uniqueness. Whether you think you're creative or not, you are! Your creativity may be best expressed in writing, music, dance, art, preparing a delicious meal, setting a beautiful table, or in an idea for a new business, a scientific breakthrough, a social movement, or the solution to a complicated problem.

Your creativity will become evident when you identify your passion. You can do so by considering what you really care about, what you really enjoy, and especially by discovering those things that make you feel totally alive and energized. You may have to learn by trial and error, and that's okay. A big clue to your passion is how you feel before, during, and after doing it.

If you dread doing something or get a headache every time you do it, it's probably not your passion. Conversely, if you can hardly wait to get started or get so into what you're doing that you lose track of time or forget to eat, your creativity is probably flowing in the area of your passion.

When you find your passion, the challenges you face will fade into the background. It doesn't mean that they aren't there; rather, it means that they are no longer the most important things on your mind. You will be better able to face all challenges with renewed energy and fresh creativity after you've spent time on your passion.

Everyone is wired differently and beautifully, and within all that wiring and inherent strengths, talents, and learned skills, are unique passions. This is where we flow. This is where we shine. This is where we fulfill the good purposes for which we were born and perfectly matched. This is where our authentic happiness and real success begin because when we're accessing our assets, we're less focused on our perceived flaws.

Make a list of your skills, talents, abilities, and strengths. Think about how you can use your unique combination of assets to work towards a goal that inspires you. Consider trying artistic expression like painting, sculpting, or crafts. Try learning to play a musical instrument or learning to dance. Try cooking, gardening, or a course on something of interest to you. For some people, their passion involves solving a problem or providing a service for others.

Humans are the only species endowed with the gift of imagination, so use your imagination to find your unique creativity. When you tap into your creativity, you will discover your passion.

You may have to experiment in different areas before you find the unique expression of your creativity, but don't let that hold you back. You may find that your experimentations in creative expression are some of the most enjoyable and rewarding times you may ever have.

How will you exercise your imagination?

Meditation

I will be creative today, putting to full use the power of my imagination, my mind, and my talents.

Actions

- I will allow my creativity to flow today. I refuse to hold back for fear of what others say or think.

- I will recall the ways that I have been creative in the past, including in my childhood.

- I will use the gift of my imagination today to find unique expressions of my creativity.

- I will evaluate the expressions of my creativity to find those things that I am passionate about.

Regardless of how long it takes, make the effort to find your creativity, because when you do, you'll find your passion, which is your best source of sustainable happiness. Your self-esteem will increase because your expression of creativity will confirm your uniqueness and value. You will be self-actualizing, which leads to a sense of fulfillment and contentedness that cannot be attained any other way.

On a scale of 1–10, 10 being highest, how would you rate your creativity? How will you increase your happiness by expressing your creativity?

DAY 28
BE PURPOSEFUL

"If you want to be happy, set a goal that commands your thoughts, liberates your energy, and inspires your hopes."
—ANDREW CARNEGIE

TO BE PURPOSEFUL is to live deliberately, with specific values that are consistent with your defined purpose for life. Purposeful living yields a life of deliberate actions that fulfill your life's purpose or move you toward fulfillment.

People who don't live purposefully are easily influenced and distracted. They rarely achieve their goal because they don't set specific goals or take any deliberate steps toward their achievement. Goals, like that of being consistently happy, are rarely achieved without deliberate, purposeful effort.

Living purposefully isn't exclusively about living a life driven by goal achievement. It also means deciding to live according to your values, and never deviating from what you believe is right. For example, if you believe that honesty and integrity are of the utmost importance in your life, living purposefully means never lying, cheating, or engaging in any other form of deceit.

People who live purposefully are deliberate about everything they say or do. Consider the purpose of every comment you make, question you ask, or action you take. Consider how your comments will make others feel before you make them. To live purposefully, ask yourself what you hope to achieve by making that statement, asking that question, or taking that action. If the statement, question, or action will hurt someone or will likely result in moving you away from your purpose, don't say or do it.

Being purposeful also involves applying a filter that helps you regulate your words and actions so that you don't do or say anything that you'll later regret. It helps you choose to say and do only those things that represent your true self, and that will, as a result, make you happier.

Know your desired outcome for everything you do. Once you are clear on your purpose, it will be easier to choose to say and do only those things that help you achieve your desired purpose.

Think about how your words and actions make other people feel. Do you leave others feeling better for having been with you?

Meditation

Today, I will make deliberate choices about the way I spend these 24 hours I've been given.

Actions

- I will be deliberate and purposeful about everything I do today.

- I will purposely try to leave people better than I find them.

- I will consider how my words or actions will make others feel before I say or do them.

Your purpose can be as simple as a daily commitment to making right choices and treating people well, or it can be as aspirational as working towards one day being the CEO of your own company.

On a scale of 1–10, 10 being highest, how would you rate your purposeful living? How will you increase your happiness by being more purposeful?

DAY 29
FAIRNESS

*"Don't cry because it's over, smile
because it happened."*
—LUDWIG JACOBOWSKI

FAIRNESS is a priceless trait. Being fair and choosing to surround yourself with people who are just and fair leads to trust, which is intrinsic to good relationships.

People who are consistently fair develop a reputation for fairness and as a result find that they attract fair and just people into their lives. They are often offered opportunities that would never be offered to a person who is not fair, such as a person who shows partiality, discriminates, or looks out only for themselves without regard for others.

The feeling of being treated unjustly is a terrible feeling. Whether it's being overlooked by a clerk who helps someone else when you've clearly been waiting longer or a much more serious injustice like being unfairly accused of a crime you didn't commit, being treated unfairly is always a bad feeling. Being treated unfairly is a direct attack on our self-esteem and our sense of control. The more serious the injustice, the more we feel like our control is being taken from us.

When we're treated fairly, we feel validated and worthy. When we treat others fairly, we are validating and affirming their worth and value. Fairness is integral to good relationships, and good relationships with good people contribute to our happiness.

Take an honest look at the times you've been treated unfairly. Forgive the people who treated you unfairly. Ask yourself how fair you've been with the people in your life. Forgive yourself for times when you've been less than fair, and determine to live with a sense of fairness and justice from today forward. When you do that, unfairness will rarely disrupt your happiness, and when it does, you will promptly deal with it and move on.

Think of a time when you were treated unfairly. How did that feel? How will you contribute to your happiness and that of others by being fair in the future?

Meditation

I will be fair in everything I do and say today.

Actions

- I will be fair in everything I do today.

- I will not show partiality to anyone.

- I will do my best to make others feel validated and affirmed.

We are happy to the degree we feel in control. It's human nature to want to feel in control. When life is unfair, we feel like we're not in control. We cannot level the playing field of life and make sure that everything is fair for us and for those with whom we're in relationship, but we can do our best to be fair in everything we say and do. When we do that, we increase our happiness as well as the happiness of those around us.

On a scale of 1–10, 10 being highest, how would you rate your fairness? How will you increase your happiness by valuing fairness?

DAY 30
SOBRIETY

"Happiness is not something you postpone for the future; it is something you design for the present."
—JIM ROHN

SOBRIETY indicates that you are ready for whatever comes your way. Sobriety contributes to clarity of mind which enables you to make the choices that will result in your happiness.

Sober people are ready to react to danger, ready to take charge if necessary, ready to lead others, and ready to accept opportunities that arise.

Conversely, people who "self-medicate" may disqualify themselves from opportunities (and never even be aware of it); they may fail to react quickly to danger, and may lead others to similarly dull their senses.

Some people mistakenly think that they need alcohol or drugs to help them relax or to get their minds off their problems. But these things don't lead to happiness. In fact, the opposite is true. If you are a leader, or want to be one, value sobriety. If you want to succeed in your personal and professional life, choose sobriety and be ready for opportunities when they arise. If you want true, sustainable happiness, replace drugs, alcohol, and anything else you use to cloud your mind with humor, laughter, healthy relationships, and all the other good things that contribute to happiness.

In addition to food, drugs, and other substances, we can become intoxicated by power, influence, money, and by infatuation with other people. We can also become intoxicated or obsessed with our aspirations, even to the point of destroying relationships so that we can be freed up to claw our way to the top.

Consider times when you haven't been sober, regardless of the source of intoxication. Consider the things that you said or did while under the influence of some substance or obsession. Would you be embarrassed or humiliated if those words or actions were seen by everyone you know? How does that make you feel?

Now consider those times when you were at your very best: clear-headed, focused, and totally on your game. How would you feel if the things you said or did at your very best were seen by everyone you know? How does that make you feel?

Meditation

I will control my impulses and maintain my complete sobriety.

Actions

- I will remain totally sober and in complete control of myself today and every day.

- I will not put any material thing, aspiration, or obsession above my relationships with the good people in my life.

- I will not become intoxicated on any substance or on any of the other things upon which people can become intoxicated.

Be aware of those things that can dull your sense or lure you away from fulfillment of your purpose. These intoxicants are lures to false happiness. Don't be fooled. Intoxication by anything will never make you truly happy. Determine to be totally alert and ready for success, and you will have eliminated a big deterrent to your happiness.

On a scale of 1–10, 10 being highest, how would you rate your sobriety? How will you increase your happiness by valuing sobriety?

CONCLUSION

Now that you've taken an honest look at your life, begin to envision yourself living the life of happiness you want to live. When a negative thought pops into your head, replace it with a positive one. (Imagine changing the thought in your mind like changing the channel on a TV.)

When a challenge presents itself, deal with it and then turn your attention back to those steps that will help you regain and maintain your happiness.

Look for ways to do good for others, because helping others leads to feelings of fulfillment and happiness that cannot be attained any other way.

Make following these 30 steps to happiness into a lifestyle. Consistent application of these steps, coupled with your willingness to be good to yourself and to others, will lead you to amazing opportunities, fulfillment of your life's purpose, and to authentic happiness in your future.

Let your happiness brighten every room you enter!

GO ON, BE HAPPY!

ABOUT THE AUTHOR

R HONDA Sciortino is an author, speaker, business owner, the founder and chairperson of Successful Survivors Foundation, and the national champion of the LOVE IS ACTION COMMUNITY INITIATIVE. She is a successful survivor of child abuse, and is a passionate advocate for children who have been abandoned, neglected, abused, and/or trafficked.

ALSO BY
RHONDA SCIORTINO

Succeed Because of What You've Been Through

Successful Survivors

How to Get to Awesome

Acts of Kindness

The Kindness Quotient